The GOODBYE THAT SAVED ME

-Ander Kesseller

This is a work of non-fiction. The names, characters, events, and experiences are drawn from real life and reflections of personal growth. Any resemblance to actual persons, living or dead, is purely coincidental unless explicitly stated.

For permission requests, write to the publisher at:
anderkesseller@gmail.com

First Edition, 2025

Disclaimer

This book is intended for educational and inspirational purposes only. It does not substitute for medical, psychological, or legal advice. The author and publisher assume no responsibility for any outcomes resulting from the application of information contained in this book.

To those who found courage to say goodbye—this is your beginning.

PREFACE

There are books that come from the mind. And then, there are books that are written by the body — through heartbreak, stillness, tears, and healing.

This is that second kind.
I didn't write this because I had answers. I wrote it because I survived the questions.

I know what it feels like to love someone so much you forget your own name. To beg for crumbs and call it connection. To disappear quietly inside something you once prayed for.

This book is my goodbye. But more importantly — it's also my return. To my voice. My worth. My wildness. To the woman I never truly lost... just silenced.

If you're holding this, maybe you're somewhere in that same ache.
This is for you.
Not to save you — but to remind you:
You already are.

— Ander Kesseler

TABLE OF CONTENT

INTRODUCTION

This isn't a love story.
It's a remembering story.

The truth is — the person I was most attached to wasn't even him. It was the version of me who believed I needed him to feel worthy.

This book traces the slow unraveling of a woman who forgot her own power... and the soft, sacred rebuild that followed.

I wrote these chapters during different seasons — some in rage, some in numbness, some in deep peace. There's no linear healing here. Just honesty.

You may cry. You may see yourself in places you didn't want to. You may finally whisper, "That's me."

That's where the healing starts.

Read this however you need to:
In one sitting, with tears. Or slowly, like medicine.
There are no rules here.
Only returnings.

Welcome home.

Before I chose myself,
I chose what hurt me — beautifully.
Because I thought love meant staying.
Even when it burned.
But all endings are mirrors.
And this one reflected my becoming.

SURRENDER

CHAPTER I
She Didn't Know She Was Disappearing

I see her now — that girl I used to be.

She's brushing her teeth next to him. Silent. Shrinking. A ghost in her own mirror.

She doesn't know she's disappearing. But I do.

She moves through rooms like a whisper — always making space, never taking it. She thinks that's love.

"If I'm softer, he'll stay." "If I ask less, he'll love me more."

And so she folds.
Like origami — beautifully broken.

She thinks she's loved because he hasn't left.

But not leaving is not the same as choosing. She doesn't know that yet.

She doesn't know love isn't about how much you bend, but how much you bloom beside someone.

I remember how she measured her worth by how quiet she could become. How many emotions she could bury before breakfast. How invisible she could be without disappearing entirely

She thought silence was strength.

She didn't realize silence is sometimes surrender — the kind that leaves your soul in ruins.

There was no big betrayal. No grand exit. Just erosion. The slow death of aliveness.

"*Why do I feel so lonely when I'm not alone?*" she whispered one night, staring at the ceiling.

She never answered. She just turned over and went back to pretending.

Back then, I didn't know it either. That we were bleeding inside something that never held us.

Love should never feel like exile. And yet, she made a home out of waiting.

She didn't cry much. Not because she wasn't hurting. But because even her pain had grown polite. There's a certain kind of grief you can't name — the grief of not being seen.

The grief of loving someone so much, you forget to love yourself.

I want to scream now:

"You are not hard to love. You are hard to manipulate. There's a difference."

But she wouldn't have heard me. Not then. She had built her identity around the idea that if she could just love harder, it would be enough.

But love shouldn't be earned through erosion. Love should meet you where you are — not where you've contorted yourself to fit.

She told herself fairytales. And then punished herself for not being magical enough to make them real.

She thought she had to choose between being loved and being whole.

I want to tell her now:

"You were never too much. You were just trying to be enough for someone who was already empty."

She gave him her light, hoping it would illuminate something between them. But he only ever stood in the glow.

Never reflected it back.

She stopped dancing in the kitchen. Stopped singing in the shower. She stopped looking herself in the eyes.

What's the word for that slow surrender of self?

It isn't heartbreak. It's hollowing.

But no one teaches us how to grieve ourselves.

She thought she could love him into becoming the man she needed. But you cannot heal someone else's absence by becoming smaller.

The truth was: she wasn't waiting for him to love her. She was waiting for her to love her. For her voice to come back. For her fire to stop apologizing for burning.

And one day... it did.

Not in a bang. But a flicker. The smallest, bravest thought:

"I don't want to live like this."

It didn't sound like rage. It sounded like awakening.

That was the moment everything began to change.

She didn't pack her bags right then. She didn't even raise her voice.

But a seed was planted.

The soil cracked. She had believed she needed his love to be whole.

What she really needed — was her own permission. Permission to outgrow the version of her that begged.

Permission to question the myth that suffering equals devotion.

Permission to stop proving and start being.

That's the thing no one tells you:

The first goodbye doesn't happen outside. It happens within.

It's the goodbye to your own self-abandonment. The goodbye to the performance.

The goodbye to the girl who thought love had to hurt to be real.

And when you say that goodbye — even quietly — the world rearranges.

You find your voice again in whispers.

You stop apologizing for asking.

You stop bargaining with your worth.

You start remembering that love is not an altar you bleed on. It's a mirror that reflects you back to yourself.

And so she began. Slowly. Softly. She read a poem one morning and cried for no reason. But there was a reason. She was thawing.

She put on lipstick just for herself.

She started listening to songs she used to love.

She texted a friend she hadn't talked to in months.

Tiny rebellions. Quiet revolutions.

Because returning to yourself doesn't always look like fire. Sometimes it looks like buying fresh flowers when no one will see them.

Sometimes it looks like whispering "*I miss you*" — to the woman in the mirror.

This chapter isn't about a breakup.

It's about an awakening. It's about the moment she realized:

"I'm not disappearing. I'm becoming."

And becoming isn't loud.

It isn't always fierce. Sometimes it's subtle. Gentle. Like dusk before the dawn.

She didn't know it then. But she was already on her way home.

She just hadn't arrived yet. And maybe neither have you. But if you're reading this — you've started walking.

And that is enough. She didn't know she was disappearing. But I do now.

And this is the book I wrote to bring her back.

It begins the moment you see yourself and whisper: "You're worth coming home to."---

---

ATTACHMENT

The Threads that held me HOSTAGE

CHAPTER 2

The Lie of Love – What They Didn't Tell Me About Attachment

"He never promised me forever. I just heard it in the way he laughed."

I wish someone had told me that love is not always a home. Sometimes it's a hotel – a temporary stay that you mistake for a forever kind of place. And then one morning, you wake up with all your bags unpacked and realize... they left.

No letter.
No apology.
Just a memory where a person used to be.

I remember being five, standing at the gate, waiting for someone who said they'd come. Maybe it was my father. Maybe a friend. Maybe the world. But no one showed up.

That day, I learned to wait. I didn't know I was also learning to attach.

"If I stay good enough, still enough, small enough — maybe they'll come."

We don't learn love from romance.
We learn it from absence.
From the silence between "*I'll be there*" and *"I'm sorry I forgot."*

And so began the quiet rehearsal of abandonment — the play I didn't audition for, but kept performing in every relationship since.

The First "Forever" I Believed In

He said, "*I'm not going anywhere.*"
But the truth is — he never really arrived.
Only his words did.

We attach not to people — We attach to the version of us that feels seen when they're around.

I loved the way I felt in his gaze —
Until one day he blinked, and I disappeared.

The Café That Knew My Secrets

There was this little café near the metro station.
Same old playlist, overused fairy lights, two teacups — one always waiting.
We used to sit there. Talk. Laugh. Play pretend.

But I went there alone one evening.
He was *"busy."*

I ordered two cups out of habit.
When the server asked, *"Should I cancel the second one?"*
I smiled and said,

"No. He'll come."

He didn't.
Neither did closure.

What a strange thing — waiting for someone who already left you in their heart, while you keep ordering tea for their ghost.

Love, they said, is a string that connects two hearts.
But nobody warned me —
Sometimes that string becomes a leash.
And you forget who you are when it tightens.

I became the girl who checked her phone like it was life support.
I tied my worth to his replies.
And every silent hour felt like a scream at my existence.

There's no bell that rings when you cross the line from loving to losing yourself. It happens in fragments. In notifications that don't come. In words you stop saying. In smiles you force.

Attachment is a Story

Attachment is not love.
It is a belief disguised as affection.

It's a desperate clinging to a story you wrote alone, hoping someone else would play their part.

"If I lose you, I lose something in me."
"If you stop choosing me, maybe I was never worth choosing."
"If I let go, I will break."

But the truth?

Letting go doesn't break you.
Holding on to what's already gone does.

Attachment is the illusion that if you hold tighter, they'll remember how to hold you.
But they won't.
And they can't.
Because you were never holding the person — only the idea of them.

"Maybe he's just tired."
"Maybe I'm expecting too much."
"Maybe this is what love feels like — patience, right?"

No
Love is not supposed to feel like waiting in a warzone, hoping the bomb won't drop.

That night I typed:

"I miss you."

Then deleted it.
Instead, I texted myself:

"Come back home. You've left yourself for too long."

Attachment as Amnesia

The problem with attachment is that it's not romantic — it's amnesia.
You forget your own name trying to memorize theirs.
You forget your own voice because you're echoing theirs.

There's no poetry in losing your soul to be kept

The Mirror of Realization

I used to think love was losing myself in someone.
Now I know —

Real love is when I find more of me with them, not less.

They didn't tell me love should feel safe.
They didn't tell me attachment is addiction wrapped in poetry.
They didn't tell me that longing is not proof of love — just proof of emptiness.

So I had to learn it the hard way.
Through silent phones, cold cafés, and empty chairs.

And more painfully —
Through the loss of myself.

No one teaches us this:
The first goodbye is not to them.
It is to the version of you who thought this was love.

You grieve not just them — But the version of you that believed suffering was sacred.

True love does not ask you to prove yourself through endurance.
It meets you.
It holds you.
It mirrors you back to yourself without distortion.

Sometimes the storms
isn`t outside its
WITHIN

CHAPTER 3
The Emotional Hijack

Nobody tells you how loud desperation can sound inside your body.
How your chest becomes a hostage.
How logic walks out quietly while longing throws a tantrum in your ribcage.

"Just text him."
"What if this time he responds?"
"Say sorry. Even if you didn't do anything."

I wasn't in love anymore.
I was in withdrawal.

And the person I was begging for – wasn't even him.
It was the version of me that felt safe when he stayed.
The version who believed being chosen meant being whole

I stared at my phone like it was a god. Checking. Rechecking. Refreshing. Obsessing..

The three dots... then nothing.
The seen tick... then silence.

"Did I say something wrong?"
"Should I not have posted that story?"

I kept looking for the mistake in myself.
Because accepting he stopped caring felt heavier than self-blame.

When I couldn't find a reason, I created one:

"It must be me."

That's how emotional hijack begins.
Not with betrayal — but with self-erasure.
Not with their silence — but our surrender to it.

The Desperation Loop

"Maybe if I explain better..."
"Maybe if I'm sweeter..."
"Maybe if I cry harder, they'll understand..."

I forgot my dignity somewhere between *"I miss you"* and *"please answer."*
It wasn't just a text. It was a cry for proof that I was still lovable.

Love didn't feel like peace. It felt like panic wearing perfume.

A beautiful agony.
A hunger that no amount of attention could feed.

What Science Says: **Hijack Is Real**

There's a name for this state: ***Amygdala Hijack.***

In moments of emotional threat — like perceived rejection or abandonment — the brain's amygdala (our survival center) goes into overdrive.

It hijacks logic.
It floods the body with stress hormones — cortisol, adrenaline.
The prefrontal cortex, the part that handles reason and boundaries, shuts down.

And in that moment — you can't think.
You can only react.

That's why I couldn't stop.
Not because I was weak.
But because I was chemically drowning in an illusion of threat.

The Puppet of My Own Longing

He didn't even have to try. I was dancing to my own fears. A puppet. Strings tied not to him — But to every childhood wound that whispered:

" *Don't be abandoned again."*
"You're nothing if you're not loved."
"Don't be too much or they'll leave."

That wasn't love.
That was trauma in a beautiful costume.
That was a little girl begging from an adult body.

I recorded a voice note at 3:12 AM.
"I know I messed up. I just... I need you to know I love you.
That I'm trying.
That I'm sorry if I pushed too hard.
I didn't mean to — I just don't know how to lose you."

I never sent it.
But I played it on loop.

Not for him.
For me.

To hear my pain outside of me — like maybe if it had a voice, it would finally be heard.

It wasn't.

Because pain doesn't need an audience.
It needs a witness — and I had abandoned myself too long to play that role.

It was 2 AM.
I called. He didn't pick up.

So I texted.
And texted.
And then texted again.

Each message more hollow than the last:

> *"I'm sorry."*
> *"I'll change."*
> *"Can we please talk?"*
> *"I need you."*
> *"Please."*

It wasn't a conversation I was begging for.
It was identity.

Because without his reflection, I didn't know if I still existed.

The next morning, I hated myself.
Not because of what he did.
But because of what I became.

A beggar.
On my knees for breadcrumbs.
Choking on silence I volunteered for.

There's a special kind of shame in realizing you handed your soul to someone who wouldn't even return a hello

Philosophy of Losing the Self

The deepest grief isn't losing them.
It's losing you in pursuit of them.

I wasn't addicted to him.
I was addicted to the feeling of being wanted.
To the story where I was finally enough.

Love should not require a blackout of dignity.
Real love doesn't ask you to forget who you are to be chosen.
That's not romance.
That's ruin.

The Psychology of Hijack

Attachment trauma doesn't scream.
It whispers:

> *"You'll never find this again."*
> *"This is the best you'll get."*
> *"You can't be alone."*

This is how the nervous system binds itself to pain — because pain is familiar. And the familiar feels safer than the unknown.

I wasn't choosing him.
I was choosing the chemical pattern — the dopamine hit, the crash, the adrenaline panic.

In neuroscience, it's called intermittent reinforcement. Random rewards, unpredictable attention — the same technique casinos use.

He became my slot machine.
And I kept pulling, hoping this time, I'd win something resembling love.

Breaking Down in Public

I was at work when the breakdown hit. All he did was leave me alone when I was in urgent need. But it was enough to flood my chest with grief.

I locked myself in a bathroom stall, held my breath, and let the tears fall silently.

> *"I'm so tired of needing him."*

But I still checked my phone.
Even through the tears.
Even while hating myself for it.

Who Are You Without The Ache?

We create an identity out of longing.
And when it leaves, so does our sense of self.

So we chase it. Not because it's right —
But because we don't know who we are without the ache
But you're not the ache.
You're the awareness underneath it.
You're not the heartbreak.
You're the healing waiting for permission.

Love didn't disappear.
It was always inside you — Buried beneath years of begging.

The Grief of Losing the Illusion

People think the breakup is the hardest part.
It's not.

It's the moment you realize:

> *"I was the only one fighting."*
> *"I kept watering a dead plant."*
> *"I begged for what should have been natural."*

That grief?
It doesn't come with closure.
It comes with mirrors.

And it doesn't end in a bang. It ends in a whisper:

"You can stop now."

One night, instead of texting him –
I opened my Notes app.

“This isn’t who you are.
You are not built to beg.
You are made of stardust, storms, and soul.
You are not unworthy because someone stopped loving you.
You are just waking up from a love that wasn’t real.
And you are allowed to come back to yourself now.”

I didn’t cry.
I didn’t shake.

I just hit save.
And that was the first time I chose me –
Not loudly, but completely.

THE SHADOW

"I disappeared not all at once, but slowly —
every time I
chose silence over truth."

CHAPTER 4

The Girl Who Forgot Herself

There was a time I could describe myself with wonder.

Favorite book? The Little Prince.
Favorite drink? Masala chai, no sugar.
Things I loved? Dancing barefoot. Rewriting quotes on napkins. Crying during thunderstorms — not because I was broken, but because it made me feel closer to something ancient and wild within me.

But somewhere between trying to be his safe place and saving a love that kept collapsing, I misplaced the girl who once answered those questions with light in her voice.

Now?

I didn't even know what music made me feel alive.
All my playlists had his fingerprints.
All my opinions came with a disclaimer: "*But I could be wrong...*"

The Room of Almosts

I was sitting on the floor, surrounded by the things that once told stories about me. A worn-out diary.

Half-read books with my handwriting in the margins.
Photos from college where my eyes still laughed —
unfiltered, unafraid.

But all I felt was distance.
Like I was standing inside a memory museum —
surrounded by relics of a girl who once felt real.

"Where did you go?" I asked the mirror.

But the girl in it looked back — tired, polite, not broken... just edited.

That's the thing about self-loss.
It doesn't happen in earthquakes.
It happens in daily silences.
In micro-forgets. In becoming agreeable.

I hadn't been stolen. I had been rewritten — line by line, smile by smile, no louder than a whisper.

The Science of Self-Abandonment

Psychology calls it fawning —

A trauma response where you suppress your needs to keep others comfortable.

It's a nervous system in survival mode.

The ventral vagal system — the part of you that fosters connection — begins to misfire. You don't feel safe unless you're agreeable.

.

So you shapeshift. To avoid abandonment, your brain rewires desire into compliance. It's not weakness. It's biology. But it costs you your soul

The Slow Unbecoming

Losing yourself doesn't happen like a scream.
It happens like this:

You delete the message you wanted to send.
You say "*It's okay*" when it's not.
You laugh at jokes that bruise you.
You stop dancing in your room because silence feels safer than your joy.

And one day, you wake up brushing your teeth, looking in the mirror –
And realize the woman looking back is tidy, composed... and gone.

It was a normal night.
Dinner with friends. He made a joke about my overthinking.
Everyone laughed.
I laughed too.

"God, you're always so sensitive," he added.

And I smiled

The kind of smile that aches in your gums.
The kind you've practiced. The kind that hides.

Later that night, I sat in the bathroom.
Lights off. Hands gripping the sink.

"Am I too much? Or have I just been too alone with my feelings for too long?"

That night,
I questioned my softness.

And that's how internalized gaslighting works: You become your own silencer

Philosophy of Remembrance

I used to think healing was forgetting him.
But it's not.
It's remembering me.

And to remember yourself...
You first have to admit that you left

"No one saved me — because I told them I didn't need saving."

That was the lie I swallowed daily.
The performance I perfected.
Smile. Numb. Comply.

Small griefs are loudest in fluorescent aisles. I reached for his favorite snack without thinking.

Then froze.

"He doesn't live here anymore."
"He never really did."
And I realized... I didn't know what I liked.
What I craved. What delighted me. What made me feel real.

Even in absence, he was still choosing for me.
Even in silence, I wasn't free.

So I left the cart.
Sat in my car.
And wept over crackers and a forgotten self.

How Identity Is Formed — and Lost

Your sense of self is built through mirroring —
Being seen, heard, and valued for who you are.

When that doesn't happen — especially in childhood —
You begin to mirror others instead.

Psychologists call it enmeshment —
When your identity fuses with another's needs, moods, desires.
You don't know where they end and you begin.
Love feels like disappearing. And disappearing feels like safety.

THE SHIFT

Here's a truth no one prints on quote cards:

You can fall in love and completely lose yourself —
Not because they took you...
But because you handed yourself over like a sacrifice.

We mistake surrender for maturity.
We call it compromise.
We wrap abandonment in bows and call it "balance."

But when you shrink to be loved, You teach your nervous system that you are only lovable in fragments.

That is not love.
That is silent self-betrayal.

Closet of Versions

One evening, I sat in front of my closet.
Not just the clothes — the identities.

Inside were all the versions I buried:

- The unapologetic me who used to argue fiercely.

- The emotional me who cried during Pixar movies.

- The dreamer who wanted to live in Paris for a year.

• The loud, weird, magical girl who didn't care about being liked.

They hadn't died.
I had just stopped inviting them to the room.

"*I'm sorry,*" I whispered.

And that was the first apology that felt holy.

Re-Invitation

Your soul never leaves.
It waits. Quietly.
At the edge of your forgetting.

It doesn't punish.
It doesn't shout.

It waits — for you to turn inward and say:

"Come back. I remember you now."

And when you do, it doesn't demand reasons.
It simply opens its arms.

That's what healing is:
The homecoming of your truest self.

Rebirth: Letter to the Forgotten Self

Dear Me,
I left you on read for years.
I dressed up as what they wanted and forgot your name.
I wore silence like a shield. I made their comfort my compass.

But I'm here now.

I remember your favorite book.
I remember how you laughed with your whole face.
I remember the way you used to dance barefoot in rain, unafraid of being seen.

I'm learning to love you again — loudly, consistently, without edits.

This time, you don't have to shrink.
You get to stay whole.

Return to the Café

I went back to that old café. Alone — but not lonely.

I ordered chai. No sugar.
My choice.

I sat where I used to sit with him.
And whispered to the wind:
"I'*m back. I'm sorry I left. But I won't leave again.*"

And for the first time in a long time,
The cup didn't tremble in my hands.

Because it was me holding it –
The real me.
The remembered me.

And she was finally ready to stay.

CHAPTER 5

Becoming My Own Home

(The Sacred Return to the Self)

There was a time I thought "*home*" was someone else's arms.
That peace was what happened when someone finally chose me.
That if I loved someone right — gently, loyally, wholly — I would be safe.

But no one told me what happens when they leave... And take your sense of worth with them.

They didn't leave me.
Not really.
I was the one who walked out on myself —
Every time I abandoned my truth to keep the peace.
Every time I made space for others but left none for me.
Every time I mistook approval for affection.
Every time I shrank so love would stay.

Coming home to myself wasn't a grand revelation. It was a

quiet, trembling choice.
One breath.
One boundary.
One honest moment at a time.

The House I Abandoned

Imagine a house.
It once had laughter spilling from its windows, sunlight dancing on the walls, shelves filled with favorite books, and floors kissed by bare feet dancing to old music.

Then slowly –
Visitors came.
Some rearranged furniture.
Some criticized the color of the walls.
Some slammed doors and called it love.

So I started dimming the lights.
Hiding the art.
Boarding up the windows.

And one day I looked around and realized:
This house didn't feel like mine anymore.

That house... was me.

The Mirror That Didn't Lie

It was an ordinary morning. No makeup. Puffy eyes. Silence. I stood in front of the mirror, expecting the old inner critic to arrive –

The one who called me "too sensitive," "too emotional," "too much."

But she didn't come.
Instead, I heard:

> "*You're still here.*
> *And that's enough.*"

No applause.
No audience.
Just a moment of truth.

I looked into my own tired eyes and, for the first time in years, didn't flinch.
Not because I looked perfect.
But because I looked real.

That was the beginning.
Not of confidence — but of intimacy with myself.

What Does It Mean to Be Your Own Home?

To be your own home is not to be perfect.
It's to be a safe place for your own truth.

It's the shift from:

- *"Will they stay if I show this part of me?"*

to

- "I will stay — even if they don't."

It's knowing:

"I can hold space for my sadness without apologizing for it." "I am not broken just because I'm still healing."
"I will not exile parts of myself to be accepted by someone else."

When you become your own home —
You stop searching for belonging in places that require you to leave yourself behind.

The First "No"

He texted.
Not "*I miss you.*"
Not "*I'm sorry.*"
Just a casual *"hey."*

The kind that reopens wounds you thought had healed.
The kind that feels like a hook disguised as harmless.

I stared at the screen.
My fingers hovered.

"*Hey, it's been a while...*"

The old me would've responded.
Grasping at crumbs.
Calling them closure.

But something inside me whispered:

"No more re-entry."
"This house is under renovation."

And for the first time — I didn't reply.
Not from anger.
But from alignment.

Saying "no" didn't feel like rebellion.
It felt like rest.

Healing didn't announce itself with fireworks.
It arrived like morning sun on a winter window.

- Making tea the way I like it — cardamom-heavy, no sugar.

- Laughing alone at a stupid meme — without needing someone to validate it.

- Playing music I hadn't heard since I left college — and remembering who I was before I started performing love.

- Sitting with loneliness like it wasn't a punishment, but a presence.

These weren't grand acts.
They were sacred rituals of return.

Moments where I chose me.
Gently. Again and again.

How Coming Home Actually Heals the Brain

It turns out —
The brain is a beautifully repairable place.

When we experience chronic abandonment (emotional or physical), the nervous system adapts for survival:

- Hypervigilance.

- People-pleasing.

- Fawn response — choosing connection over truth.

But healing is possible.
Through neuroplasticity, we can rewire the brain to feel safe inside our own presence.

Every time I sat in discomfort without self-abandoning...
Every time I chose silence over begging...
Every time I spoke my truth, even shakily... ...my nervous system learned:

> *"We're not in danger anymore."*
> *"We can stay."*

And so I stayed.

Dialogue with the Old Me

I sat on the kitchen floor one night and imagined her — The version of me who begged. Who cried over seen texts and whispered apologies she didn't owe.

I said to her:

> *"You were doing your best.*
> *You just wanted to be chosen."*

She looked up, teary-eyed.

Then I said:

> *"But now...*
> *We choose ourselves.*
> *Again.*
> *And again.*
> *And again."*

She smiled.
And for the first time, I felt both of us exhale.

The Repainting

Coming home to yourself isn't glamorous.
It's gritty. Messy. Slow.

At first, I repainted my soul in beige —
Safe colors. Quiet ones.
I wore what was "*normal.*" Spoke in palatable tones.

But then one day, I woke up and bought yellow paint.
Loud. Sunny. Unapologetic.

I hung old art.
Deleted old chats.
Burned the letters I once read like scripture.
And danced barefoot to Sufi music.

Not for aesthetics.
Not for performance.

But because I wanted to.

And that was reason enough.

The Box of Old Things

I found the box in the back of my wardrobe.
It still smelled like him.
Or maybe it just smelled like who I used to be.

Photos. Letters. That hoodie I used to sleep in.
A perfume bottle that was mostly air now.

For a second, I held it all to my chest.
The ache was familiar.
It almost felt like comfort.

But I didn't cry.

Instead, I folded everything gently.
Closed the box.
Tied it shut.

And whispered:

"Thank you for the love. Thank you for the lessons. But I live here now. Without you."

Closure doesn't always come with tears.
Sometimes, it comes with tenderness.

What Healing Journeys Often Forget to Say

Every powerful story of healing — whether in books, therapy rooms, or whispered between friends — often points to the same truth:

That coming home to yourself is the real journey.
That peace isn't found in fixing others, but in learning to stay with your own soul.

But what these stories often don't say...
is that the return to self isn't magical.
It's maintenance.

It's the quiet work of choosing your truth when no one claps. It's the courage to forgive yourself for begging. It's building boundaries without guilt — even when they call it selfish.

Coming home isn't a destination.
It's a daily devotion.
A practice of not leaving yourself again.

Why the Body Stores Breakups

The vagus nerve — the body's main emotion-processing highway — links heartbreak with physical symptoms.

That's why:

- Your chest physically aches.
- Your gut feels off.
- Your voice trembles.

It's not *"just in your head."*
It's in your whole system.

But here's the beauty:
With time, self-regulation rewrites the body's memory.

By choosing quiet, solitude, and truth —
You signal: *"I'm safe now."*

The more you choose you,
The more your body stops bracing for abandonment.

Inner Dialogue: The New Promises

"I will not shrink to be loved."
"I will not confuse pain with passion."
"I will not build altars out of old texts."
"I will belong to myself — even if no one else understands."

Because home isn't four walls.
It's a knowing.
A warmth.
A commitment to no longer walk out on yourself.

One evening, the power went out. No light. No noise. Old me would've panicked. Called someone. Searched for a hand to hold. But this time? I lit a candle. Brewed tea. Wrapped myself in a shawl. And sat near the window. Outside: silence. Inside: stillness.

And I whispered: "*I used to fear the dark. But now I understand — That's where I found the light.*"

Healing didn't arrive as a miracle.

It arrived as me — Making one right choice at a time.
Unlearning shame.
Relearning myself.
It was slow. It was sacred.
And it was mine.

I became my own home.
And this time, I won't move out again

CHAPTER 6

Boundaries Are Bridges Back to Me

People say boundaries are walls.

I disagree.

They're bridges — leading me back to myself every time I start walking too far into someone else's chaos.

The First Boundary I Ever Set

He texted again.
A voice note — soft, charming, pulling.

"I was just thinking about you. Miss our talks."

The old me would've melted.
Typed back.
Cracked open.

But this time — I paused. Took a deep breath. And said to myself:
"You don't owe access to people who once used your love as convenience."

I didn't reply.
Not out of ego.
But because I knew:
Love without respect is still abandonment.
And I was no longer available for that.

The Doormat vs. The Door

For years, I was a doormat.
Soft, sweet, available.

"*Come in,*" I'd say.
Even when I was bleeding.

But then I realized — a door can still be kind.
But it has a lock.
A choice.
A handle only I can turn.

That's what boundaries are:
Not rejection.
But self-respect with structure.

Why Saying "No" Feels So Hard

Our brains are wired for connection. The amygdala — the fear center of the brain — lights up when it senses rejection.

So setting a boundary can feel like danger, not because it is, but because our biology still fears being exiled from the tribe.

But this isn't a survival threat anymore.
This is you unlearning the belief that love must mean sacrifice.

You're not pushing them away.
You're pulling yourself back in.

When They Called Me "Selfish"

"*You've changed,*" he said.
I smiled.
Because yes — I had.

"*You used to be so... understanding.*"

Translation:

"I liked it better when I could hurt you without consequence."

He didn't miss me.
He missed the version of me that didn't honor herself.

And for the first time,
I didn't rush to fix his discomfort.

Because people who benefit from your lack of boundaries will always call your healing selfish.

The Guilt Trap

"Maybe I'm being too harsh."
"What if they think I don't care?"
"Maybe just one last time..."

Pause. Breathe.

"Would I let someone I love be treated like this?"

If the answer is no — then why not love yourself the same way?

Boundaries aren't cruelty.
They are clarity.
And clarity is love — for both of you.

The Overflowing Cup

A friend asked why I'd become *"distant."*

I said:
"I'm not distant. I'm just done bleeding every time someone touches me."

Imagine a cup.

If I keep pouring into others without filling myself, eventually I hand them an empty glass — and start tearing off pieces of my soul to keep the cup full.

No more. From now on, I pour only from overflow.

The Cost of Always Saying Yes

Chronic people-pleasing isn't kindness — it's an adaptive survival response.

When we associate love with approval, we trade authenticity for attachment.

Each time we say "yes" against our will,
we disconnect from the self we're supposed to protect.

Boundaries reconnect us.
They return us to the seat of self-respect.

The Garden Fence

I am a garden now.
Wild, soft, full of life.

But every garden needs a fence.

Not to keep people out —
but to protect the flowers that take so long to bloom.

If you love me, you'll respect the fence.
You'll wait at the gate.
You'll ask before stepping in with muddy shoes.

And if you don't —
you were never here to love. Just to take.

Saying "No" Without an Explanation

He asked:

"Wanna meet? Just talk like old times?"

I said:
"No."

Not: *"No, I'm busy."*
Not: *"No, I'm still healing."*

Just:

"No."

Because "no" is a complete sentence.

And the version of me who used to over-explain her pain... she's finally resting now.

Dialogue With My Old Self

"I know you want to keep everyone happy. I know you think love means giving endlessly. But what if you deserve to be full, too?"

What if the people meant for you will never ask you to shrink?
What if protecting your peace is the greatest act of love you've ever done?

When I Watched Someone Leave (And Didn't Chase)

They didn't like the new me.
The one who said "no."
The one who didn't beg, explain, or chase.

So they left.
And I let them.

I didn't shrink.
I didn't write a final paragraph.
I didn't perform grief.

I stayed still.

Because now I knew:
Anyone who leaves because you chose yourself...
was never choosing you to begin with.

Emotional Healing Truth

Most healing journeys aren't about learning something new — they're about remembering.

Remembering that you're not meant to be on call for chaos.
That peace is not selfish.
That loving yourself isn't rebellion — it's restoration.

And boundaries are your daily ritual of remembering

I made dinner.
Lit a candle.
Sat at the table — alone.

Not waiting. Not hoping. Not checking my phone.
Just me.
My plate.
My peace.

And I whispered:

> *"This is what love looks like now.*
> *Boundaried. Whole. Sacred."*

No longer a doormat. No longer a rescue mission.

Just a woman who finally came home — and locked the door behind her

---

You dont have to **BLEED** TO BE

WORTHY

Of being held

CHAPTER 7
Learning to Receive Love Without Earning It

There was a time I believed love was a reward.

For being good.
For staying quiet.
For carrying their pain and never dropping it.

I learned to perform love like it was a stage play.
Smiling when I wanted to cry.
Saying "*it's okay*" when I was breaking.
Being useful. Being needed. Being pleasing.

I didn't want love.
I wanted to deserve it.

The Applause That Never Came

He once said, "*You're amazing. You always know how to make me feel better.*"

I wore that as a medal.
Even when I was falling apart.
The day he left, I sat on the floor and thought:

"But I was good.
I did everything right."

That's when I realized –
I had treated love like a paycheck.
Do the work. Meet the quota. Get chosen.

But love... isn't a salary.
It's a gift.

Conditional Love Is a Lie

Real love doesn't arrive with a scoreboard.

It doesn't say:

- *"Only if you stay easy to handle."*
- *"Only if you stay convenient."*
- *"Only if you make me feel strong."*

Real love says:
"You're messy today. That's okay. I'm not leaving."

But I had never stayed long enough in anyone's arms to test that.
Because I thought the second I stopped performing, they'd walk away.

So I stayed in character.
And forgot who I was without the costume

The Love Performer

I was the actress. Always smiling. Always supportive. Always light.

Even when my insides felt like a room on fire.

I clapped for their dreams.
Wiped their tears.
Became their safe space.

But no one asked where I went when the curtains closed.

The Therapy Realization

My therapist asked:

"What does love feel like?"

I said:
"Safe. Soft. Unconditional."

She paused.
"When have you felt that?"

Silence.

I hadn't.

Not fully.
Not without effort.

Not without earning it first.

And that's when it hit me like a tidal wave:

I didn't know how to receive love.
Only how to work for it.

The Fear of Receiving

"If they give me something, I owe them back."
"If they love me too easily, maybe it's fake."
"If I didn't bleed for it, is it even real?"

These weren't thoughts.
They were programming.

I'd been conditioned to equate love with pain.
With work.
With proving.

So when softness came... I flinched.

The Day I Let Love In

He brought me flowers.
Not because I asked.
Not to say sorry.
Just... because.

I panicked. *"You didn't have to,"* I blurted.
"*It's too much. You shouldn't spend money on me...*"

He held my hand, gently.

"It's not too much. You're not too much."

And I cried. Because my nervous system didn't know how to hold something that didn't arrive with warning signs.

But I stayed. I received. I said *"thank you"* — and meant it

Why We Reject Healthy Love

When your nervous system is wired for chaos, peace feels boring.
When love was always something you chased, being chosen feels suspicious.
That's why many of us sabotage safe love. Because our blueprint says:

"Love is something you earn. Not something you're simply worthy of."

But you are.
You always were.

The Open Hand

Imagine love like an open hand.
But I used to offer it like a closed fist. Tight. Gripping. Scared.

"Please take it. Please stay. Please see me."

Now?

I open my hand.
Not begging.
Just being.

If someone holds it — welcome.
If not — I don't chase.
Because I trust now:

What's meant for me doesn't need to be wrestled with.

Rewriting the Script

He said:

"You don't have to do anything for me to stay."

I paused. And asked: "*Not even heal you?*"

He laughed softly. "*You're not my therapist. You're my person.*"

That's when I knew:

The love I deserve doesn't ask me to fix anyone to feel valuable.
It lets me just be.

Mini Moments of Receiving Without Guilt

- Letting someone carry my bag — without apologizing.
- Saying "*thank you*" instead of "*sorry I'm a mess.*"
- Letting them comfort me — without explaining my tears.
- Accepting compliments — without deflecting.

I didn't need to earn it anymore. I just needed to believe I was already worthy.

The New Belief

"I don't have to earn love. I just have to be present enough to receive it."
"I'm not too much. I was just surrounded by people who never made space."
"From now on, I choose only the love that feels like rest."

The Soft Rest

I lay in bed, head on his chest.
Breathing in sync. No words. No performance. No earning.

And in that stillness, I whispered to myself:

> *"So this is love.*
> *Not the one I bled for.*
> *But the one I grew into."*

I know you want to know who the "he" now. I will let you in next chapter....

you didn't just survive it. You became someone you actually like

CHAPTER 8
The Goodbye That Finally Meant Hello

There are some goodbyes that leave you shattered.

And then there are others that leave you still.

Not broken, not bleeding.

Just... still. Whole. Returned.

That's the kind of goodbye this was.

Opening: A Still Goodbye

I ran into him one afternoon. The ex. The ache. The unfinished sentence in a language I no longer spoke.

He looked the same.
Maybe a little older. Still charming. Still the echo of a boy who never became the man I needed.

"*You look good,*" he said.

I smiled gently, not out of habit, but out of truth.

"*I am.*"

And for the first time, I wasn't pretending.
No tight chest.
No sharp inhale.
No silent begging for closure.

Just breath.
Just presence.
Just peace.

The Man Who Didn't Feel Like a Lesson

When I met the man who would become my husband, I didn't fall.

I didn't spin.
I didn't lose myself in a whirlwind.

I grew.

There was no drama.
No danger disguised as chemistry.
No pretending.

He felt like still water — honest, safe, and grounding. He once told me,

"I'm not here to fix you. I'm here to build with you."

And I believed him. Because he didn't see me as a project. He saw me as a partner. This wasn't a rescue. This was a return.

A Garden, Not a Fire

My past loves had been wildfires — beautiful, brief, and utterly destructive.

They burned bright. And then left me in smoke and silence.
But this love? This was a garden.

Slow. Steady. Intentional.

We watered it. Together. Daily.

We pulled the weeds with compassion.
We grew things — truth, laughter, rituals, dreams.

He never needed me to shrink. He just asked me to show up. As I was. And that was enough.

The Night I Realized "This Is Different"

It was a quiet evening.

We were budgeting.
Just talking through savings, bills, goals.

No music. No candles. No staged romance.

And I looked up from the spreadsheet... and saw him.
Focused. Respectful. Collaborative. And something clicked.

"This is love too," I thought. *"Not the kind that sweeps you*

off your feet, but the kind that holds your feet on the ground."

We didn't argue to win.

We solved to grow.
We didn't talk over each other.
We listened to build.

And in that simplicity, I realized how far I'd come — and how much further I could go, with someone who didn't make me feel small to feel close.

Emotional Growth: I Didn't Have to Perform

There was a time I believed love was a reward for obedience.

Be easy. Stay small. Smile on cue.

I mastered that version of me —
the one who could disappear inside someone else's needs
and call it devotion.

But this time... I stayed.

With my tears.
With my triggers.
With my truth.

I cried — and didn't apologize for it.

I grew quiet — and didn't force a smile.
I got angry — and didn't fear abandonment.

Not because someone else gave me permission.
But because I had finally stopped walking out on myself.

That's emotional growth.
Not becoming invincible —
but becoming visible, even in your mess.
I still have wounds.

Still flinch when softness arrives too easily.
Still overthink simple acts of love.

But now, I pause.

I don't spiral. I self-soothe.
I don't shut down. I speak gently.
I don't beg to be understood. I offer myself grace first.

This love — the one I live now — isn't perfect.
But neither am I pretending anymore.

From Surviving to Expanding

We didn't just share dreams — we structured them.
Built systems.
Talked strategy.
Chose stability not as a cage, but as a canvas.

He encouraged my wildest ideas,
but more importantly — I began trusting them too.

For the first time, I wasn't building alone.

I wasn't convincing someone of my vision.
I was co-creating a life where both our lights could rise.

From scarcity to sustainability.
From survival mode to sacred momentum.
From hoarding energy to sharing abundance.

He didn't rescue me.
He respected me.

The Truest Goodbye

In truth, the man I ran into that day wasn't the real goodbye.

He was just a symbol. A mirror. A flicker of a past life.
The real goodbye was internal.

It was to the girl who:

- Called chaos "love"
- Took silence as safety
- Thought suffering made her worthy
-

I didn't abandon her.
I held her hand.

.

Told her thank you.
And gently... let her rest.

Because she got me here.
Because she carried me when I couldn't walk.

But I'm walking now.
And she's finally free

Practices That Helped Me to Love Myself

(A Ritual Guide for the Soft Return)

This is not a "how-to."
This is a remembering.

A remembering that healing isn't a finish line —
It's a rhythm. A breath. A whisper.
It's the ordinary moments where you choose you again.

These rituals didn't heal me all at once.
They met me where I was.
Some days, I was too tired to do more than whisper my own name.

But they kept me anchored.
Kept me soft.
Kept me facing inward — gently, honestly.

So here they are —
The everyday practices that helped me return to myself.

Morning Grounding Whisper

Before the world gets loud, meet yourself in stillness.

Place one hand on your heart, the other on your belly.
Breathe in for 4, hold for 4, exhale for 6.

Then softly whisper:
"I am here. I am whole. I am enough —
as I am."

You don't have to feel it yet.
You're just planting seeds.

The Candle of Closure

When letting go — a person, a pattern, a past version of you — light a candle.

Watch it burn slowly.
Say aloud or silently:

"Thank you for what you taught me. I release you now."

Let the wax carry your grief.
Let the flame carry your freedom.

Stillness Check-In (Midday Pause)

Set a timer for 3-5 minutes.
No distractions. Just you and your breath.

Ask yourself:

"What am I feeling?"
"What do I need right now?"

No need to fix anything.
The healing is in the noticing.

Mirror Ritual (Eye Contact with the Soul)

Stand in front of the mirror.
Not to fix. Not to assess. Just to witness.
Look into your eyes and say:
"I am proud of you."
"I'm sorry for abandoning you."
"I'm choosing you now — and again tomorrow."

Stay until the words feel like they're sinking in.

Nightly Softening

As the day ends, bring your hands over your chest.
Close your eyes and say:
"Today, I tried.
Today, I showed up — even if quietly.
That is enough."
Let this be your lullaby —
A permission to rest without guilt

Final Whisper

These rituals are not about discipline.

They are about devotion.

Not another task on your to-do list —

But a reminder:

You're allowed to belong to yourself

now.

Again.

And again.

And again.

Welcome home, love.

You made it back.

I AM the
CREATOR
my LIFE

Final Note: Not a Happy Ending — A Healthy Beginning

This love I live now?
It doesn't break me.
It doesn't make me prove myself.

It meets me where I am.

And for the first time, I'm writing a love story that doesn't end in heartbreak — but begins in wholeness.

Last Thoughts: From My Heart to Yours

If you've made it to the final page of this book, I already know something about you.
You've loved deeply — and maybe lost yourself in the process.

You've stayed longer than you should have, hoping love would change.
You've cried quietly in places that never saw your tears.
But still... you're here.
Healing. Growing. Becoming.
And that matters.

I didn't write this book as a story of sorrow.

I wrote it as a map home.

To show you that goodbye is not the end.

It's the doorway back to you.

This Is Your Permission Slip

- To stop performing for love
- To set boundaries that protect your peace
- To say "no" without guilt
- To walk away from what doesn't hold you gently
- To believe, deeply, that you are worthy — just as you are

If your heart still aches, if you're still unraveling — that's okay. Healing isn't perfect. It's honest.
And one day, without warning, you'll look at yourself and realize:

You didn't just survive them.
You found yourself again.
You became your own safe place.
You became free.

So here's what I hope for you, love:

May your self-respect become louder than your fear.
May your boundaries feel like grace, not guilt.
May your next chapter be chosen by you, not survival.
And may you never again shrink to be loved.

You are the home you were always searching for.

With all my heart, Goodbye That Saved Me
— From Attachment to Freedom

Letter to the Girl I Once Was

My Love,

I know you tried so hard. You stayed longer than your spirit could handle. You loved through silence, confusion, absence. You gave more than you had — again and again — thinking maybe this time, they'll see you. Choose you.

Stay. I know how tired you were. How often you cried in secret, convincing yourself you were just "too sensitive." How you learned to smile through the ache and keep the world from seeing your unraveling.

You were not weak. You were just loving with your whole heart in a place that didn't know how to hold it. And I'm sorry. For all the times I ignored your boundaries. For every night I silenced your scream just to keep peace. For treating your softness like it was something to apologize for. But I want you to know... I see you now. Not as a version to be ashamed of — but as the warrior who survived.

The one who kept believing in love, even when it bruised her. The one who planted seeds in soil that never gave back, yet still found a way to bloom. You weren't broken, my love. You were just building strength in silence.

Thank you for not giving up on us. Thank you for holding the line when everything in you wanted to disappear. You are the reason I am free.

I love you. I carry you. And I'll never abandon you again.

With reverence,
The Woman You Grew Into

Loved This Book?

If **The Goodbye That Saved Me** touched your heart, made you feel seen, or gave you strength in any way —
please take a moment to leave a review on **Amazon.**
Your words help this book reach someone who may need it most.

It only takes a minute, but it means the world.

➻ Leave a Review on Amazon

Thank you for reading. Thank you for healing.
With all my heart,

– Ander Kesseller

"You're allowed to begin again.

You always were."

www.ingramcontent.com/pod-product-compliance
Lightning Source LLC
Chambersburg PA
CBHW062144160726
48282CB00027B/933
* 9 7 8 9 3 3 4 3 4 0 5 3 2 *